MY FRIEND has Diabetes

BY ANNA LEVENE

Chrysalis Education

Distributed in the United States by
Smart Apple Media
1980 Lookout Drive
North Mankato, MN 56003

Copyright © Chrysalis Books PLC 2003

ISBN 1-93233-326-6
Library of Congress Control Number 2003102562

Editorial Manager: Joyce Bentley
Senior Editor: Sarah Nunn
Project Editor: Sue Nicholson
Designer: Wladek Szechter
Photographer: Michael Wicks
Picture Researcher: Terry Forshaw
Illustrations: Tom Connell

Consultant: Debbie Hammond, Diabetes U.K.
Diabetes U.K. is a charity working for the 1.4 million people in the U.K. with diabetes.

The photographer and publishers would like to thank Kavi Amin; Angela Carte; Ron Davies; Jane McHale; Alka, Jayesh, Prina and Priyen Patel; James Pearson; Charu and Shil Shah; David Schueler; and the Pinn Medical Centre for their help in preparing this book.

Picture acknowledgements:
26, Mediscan; 28 (left), Shaun Botterill/Getty Images; 28 (right) Dick Luria/Getty Images

Printed in Hong Kong

10 9 8 7 6 5 4 3 2 1

Contents

*Words in **bold** are explained in the glossary on page 30.*

My friend Sunil

Hello! My name is Ahmed and I'm ten years old. I live with my mom and dad and my cat, Smudge. My best friend is Sunil. He lives on the same road and we play together nearly every day.

At weekends, we often go to the park. We usually play soccer or race each other on our bikes. Sunil is really fast, so he usually wins. I don't mind too much because it's great being able to do things together again. Last summer was very different. Sunil suddenly started feeling tired and ill all the time. He was always thirsty and had to go to the bathroom a lot, too. He didn't want to play, and if we watched television he often fell asleep. It was no fun at all.

Sunil's mum began to worry about him and took him to the doctor. Dr. Fry asked Sunil about his **symptoms** and tested his blood. Soon after, Dr. Fry told them that Sunil had diabetes. That was why he was feeling so bad.

Opposite: **Sunil (in the blue T-shirt) and Ahmed practise passing shots in Sunil's garden.**

People with undiagnosed diabetes feel very thirsty all the time.

DIABETES FACTS

HOW DIABETES MAKES YOU FEEL

Before treatment, diabetes makes you feel
- Thirsty all the time, however much you drink
- Like you want to go to the bathroom, even when you've just been.
- Tired and weak

It can also cause you to lose weight and make things look blurred.

How diabetes develops

Diabetes develops when a part of the body, called the **pancreas**, stops working properly. One of the jobs of the pancreas is to make sure that we always have exactly the right amount of a sugar, called **glucose**, in our blood. If this level of sugar is wrong, we won't have enough energy to think, run, grow, or even sleep.

When we eat, some of our food is turned into glucose. The glucose leaves our stomach and goes into our blood. Our blood already contains some glucose, so when this extra glucose arrives, it suddenly has too much. A normal pancreas reacts by making and sending a messenger, called **insulin**, around our body. The insulin acts like a key to unlock cells and let in the glucose. The glucose is used by the **cells** for energy.

If somebody has diabetes, the pancreas does not send insulin around the body. The cells are not unlocked and extra glucose stays in the blood. The person with diabetes gets more and more tired because no energy is being made from the glucose. Instead, the body tries to lower the glucose by passing it out into the **urine**. This is why people with untreated diabetes go to the bathroom a lot.

They also feel very thirsty because such a lot of liquid is being lost from their bodies.

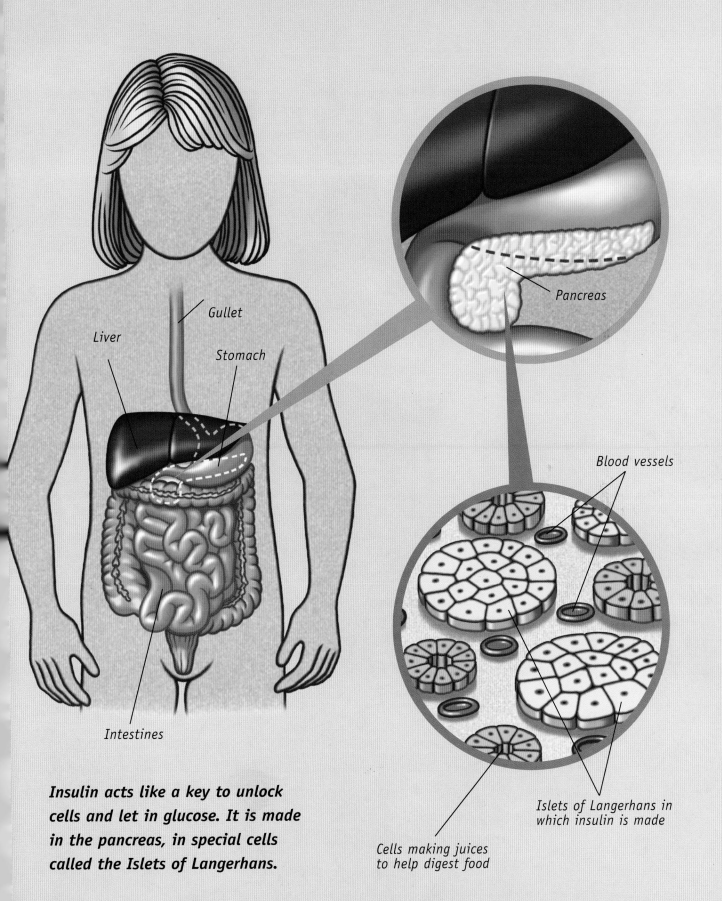

Gullet

Liver

Stomach

Pancreas

Blood vessels

Intestines

Islets of Langerhans in which insulin is made

Cells making juices to help digest food

Insulin acts like a key to unlock cells and let in glucose. It is made in the pancreas, in special cells called the Islets of Langerhans.

Injecting insulin

Sunil injects himself in a different spot each time so that no place gets sore.

Dr. Fry told Sunil and his mum that Sunil needed insulin to make him feel better.

"Your body can't make its own insulin any more, Sunil, so you, or your mom or dad, will have to **inject** insulin into your body instead. It seems scary but we'll help you get used to it.

"You'll need two injections of insulin a day, one before breakfast and one before supper.

"The insulin will lower the amount of glucose in your blood," Dr. Fry told Sunil, "so when you eat foods which turn to sugar, the level of sugar in your blood will be just right."

Sunil told me that he was too scared to inject himself at first, so his mom did it. But after a while, he realized that if he didn't learn, he wouldn't be able to stay the night with friends, or go on school trips. So he tried, and it didn't really hurt at all.

Sunil's injector looks a bit like a cartridge pen. He likes it because it doesn't have a big needle like a **syringe**.

"Where today?" he wonders.

"Your bottom?" I joked.

"No. Did that yesterday. Time for my thigh, I think."

Sunil pushes the "nib" into his skin and presses down the plunger. I didn't like watching when he first started doing it, but Sunil says it's no worse than a pin prick.

Sunil uses a pen injector like this to take insulin. Sometimes syringes with fine needles are used.

DIABETES FACTS

GROWING PROBLEM

About 17 million Americans have diabetes, and a third of these don't know they have it. It's the second most common chronic disease in children after asthma.

Visiting Uncle Rajiv

On Saturday afternoons Sunil and I often visit his Uncle Rajiv. He lives on the other side of the park.

Sometimes Uncle Rajiv asks us to get his shopping for him. He doesn't like walking too far because his feet often hurt. He says this is because of his diabetes. Uncle Rajiv became diabetic two or three years ago when his

Uncle Rajiv keeps his diabetes under control by carefully choosing what he eats and taking tablets every day.

pancreas started producing less insulin. Now he has to take tablets every day to help his body make better use of the insulin it does still produce.

When we get back from the shops, Uncle Rajiv gives us a drink of milk and an apple or banana. Before he became diabetic, he used to offer us samosas, home-made sweets, or creamy puddings. Now Uncle Rajiv has cut down on fried and sugary foods. His doctor has told him it's important he eats a healthier diet. After our snack, we often stay and play cards with him.

*Opposite: **Sunil and Ahmed bring home Uncle Rajiv's shopping. Uncle Rajiv now eats more fresh fruit and vegetables to keep himself healthy.***

DIABETES FACTS

TYPE 1 AND 2 DIABETES

Over three-quarters of all people with diabetes have **Type 2 diabetes**. This means that the pancreas still makes insulin but the body cannot use it properly. Most people with Type 2 diabetes take tablets instead of having injections and exercise is an important part of their treatment. Children usually develop **Type 1 diabetes**. This means that the pancreas does not produce any insulin at all. Most children with Type 1 diabetes have insulin injections.

Most people with Type 2 diabetes do not inject themselves. They take tablets instead.

Getting enough glucose

When Sunil injects himself with insulin, it unlocks the cells that allow his body to use glucose for energy. So Sunil has to make sure he has enough glucose in his blood, but not too much. He does this by trying to eat foods that give him glucose steadily throughout the day, and not eating lots of sweet, sugary foods.

On Saturdays, Sunil sometimes spends the night at my house. For supper, Mom often serves pizzas, with potatoes or spaghetti. These contain lots of **carbohydrates**. My favourite dessert is ice cream and chocolate sauce, but when Sunil's here we have ice cream and fruit. Sunil can still eat sweet things, but he isn't supposed to have them too often.

Sunil usually has something to eat at bedtime. His body still uses glucose while he's asleep, so he needs to make sure he has enough to last through the night.

Before bed, Sunil usually eats a bowl of cereal to top up the glucose in his blood.

Opposite: **Ahmed's mom makes sure supper is based on carbohydrates. Sunil and Ahmed both love food served on toast!**

DIABETES FACTS

A HEALTHY DIET

All diabetics should make sure they eat a healthy diet—and everyone else should, too. Try to eat something from each of these four food groups every day:

- carbohydrates (cereals, rice, potatoes, pasta, and bread)
- fresh fruit and vegetables
- **proteins** (meat, fish, eggs, peas, and beans)
- dairy foods (milk, cheese, and yoghurt)

Potatoes, pasta, and rice are all full of carbohydrates, which release glucose into the blood.

Feeling wobbly

Sunil has a sugary drink to boost his glucose levels and stop him having low blood sugar.

Once, when Sunil came to stay, Dad came home late with the shopping and didn't start making supper until seven o'clock. Sunil and I decided to play soccer in the garden until it was ready, but after about twenty minutes Sunil said he felt wobbly and had to sit down. I was worried and called Dad.

"Sunil's really shaky," I said.

"It's OK," said Sunil. "I'm just having **hypoglycemia**. I need something sugary to eat."

I rushed into the kitchen to fetch him a chocolate bar. It made him feel a bit better almost straightaway. But Sunil said he still felt funny, so Mom made him a cheese sandwich. After about quarter of an hour, he felt fine again.

"I'm starving, he said. "That chicken smells great!"

Now whenever Sunil comes to stay, we try to make sure meals are on time. Sunil has to eat at regular intervals so that the glucose level in his blood doesn't get too low. If a meal is going to be late, Mum makes sure Sunil has a snack to keep him going. At bedtime, he keeps some glucose tablets nearby in case he needs to top up his glucose level fast.

If Sunil needs to top up his sugar levels fast, he eats some cookies or a chocolate bar, or has a sweet drink. These all contain lots of sugar.

DIABETES FACTS

HAVING HYPOGLYCEMIA

The word "hypoglycemia" means that a person's body is sending warning signals to the brain that there isn't enough glucose in their blood.

Hypoglycemia makes different people feel different things. Some people feel cold, or hot, or sick, or very tired. Their hands and mouth might go tingly or they might find it hard to see properly. They might even get cross or start crying. If a diabetic friend says they're feeling strange, make them sit down and give them a fizzy drink or some chocolate. Once they start feeling better, give them something starchy to eat like a sandwich, or a bowl of cereal.

Eating glucose candy is a quick way to raise blood glucose levels.

At school

Sometimes, Sunil has a cookie on his way to school to keep up his glucose levels.

Sunil and I walk together to school every morning. On the way, we sometimes stop to buy a drink or a snack. I usually get potato chips and some lemonade. Sunil gets a diet cola and a cereal bar.

Soon after Sunil found out he had diabetes, a special nurse came to our school. She explained what diabetes was, and told us how to help if Sunil began to feel ill during a class. Now everyone knows he has to have a snack during the morning, and another during the afternoon. Before the diabetes nurse came, some children said it was unfair and they wanted to eat cookies and sandwiches then, too. Now they understand Sunil has to eat them to stay well.

If Sunil starts to feel weak and wobbly, one of us fetches a teacher straightaway.

All the teachers know they must give Sunil chocolate, cookies or glucose tablets to stop him having a hypo.

A nurse came into school to talk about diabetes to the children and teachers.

DIABETES FACTS

JUST THE SAME

If there are diabetic children in your school, don't treat them differently from your other friends. They may already feel shy and embarrassed about being given extra snacks. Most people with diabetes just want to get on with their lives without any bother.

Our favorite sports

Sunil and I love sports. In the summer, we have swimming lessons at the local pool. On the way, Sunil always has a carton of juice and a sandwich he brings from home. On the way back, he often has another snack. He uses up so much energy swimming he needs the extra carbohydrates.

During the lesson, the teacher divides us into pairs and tells us to swim close together. Then if anyone gets into difficulties, there is someone nearby to help. Sunil and I usually swim together and race each other down the pool.

We like athletics, too. Sunil's better than me at running, but I usually beat him at long jump. Once, when Sunil was running in a relay race, he nearly collapsed. He'd forgotten to eat a snack.

Mr. Finch, our teacher, gave Sunil three glucose tablets, but they didn't seem to help. Sunil still felt sick and dizzy. So, after a few minutes, Mr. Finch gave him three more. Luckily these did work—although Sunil ate a sandwich as well, just to be on the safe side.

*Opposite: **Sunil is a fast runner—and he knows that exercise is good for him.***

Sunil forgot to have a snack before the sports lesson. Now he feels sick and dizzy. He needs to eat something sugary before he has a hypo.

DIABETES FACTS

EXERCISE AND HEALTH

Everyone needs to exercise to stay healthy. Exercise is especially important for diabetics because it helps to control the amount of sugar in the blood and prevent them from becoming overweight.

Checking blood

I often go to Sunil's house after school. Before we eat, Sunil tests his blood. This shows whether he has too much or too little glucose in his blood.

Sunil washes and dries his hands, then pricks the side of his finger with a special small lancet. He squeezes out a drop of blood and puts it on a test strip in his **blood glucose meter**.

After a few seconds, a number appears in the window on the meter. Sunil told me the meter reading should be between 4 and 7. If the number is below 4, there's too little glucose in Sunil's blood. Then his mom gives him two

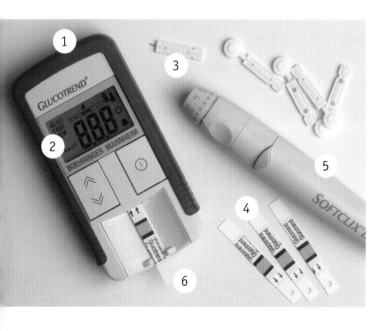

1   Blood glucose meter
2   Display screen (reading appears here when a test strip is fed into the meter)
3   Lancet, or finger-pricking device
4   Strips for blood
5   Finger-pricking device for taking blood
6   Test strip being fed into meter

Here is some of the equipment used to test glucose levels.

teaspoonfuls of sugar in milk, or a sweet fizzy drink.

If the reading is over 10, there's too much glucose in Sunil's blood. Usually this is nothing to worry about. Sunil might have eaten a large lunch, or had some glucose tablets to prevent a hypo. If however, the meter reading is over 10 several times in a week, it probably means that Sunil's insulin **dose** is not quite right. Sunil's mom must then go and see Sunil's diabetes care team to find out if the dose needs to be increased.

Sunil writes down the day's reading in his record book, and we have supper.

Opposite: **Sunil uses his blood glucose meter to test his glucose levels.**

If Sunil has too little glucose in his blood, he usually drinks some cola to raise his glucose level.

DIABETES FACTS

TESTING GLUCOSE LEVELS

It's very important that diabetics control how much glucose is in their blood. If they allow glucose levels to remain high, they may have serious health problems later on in life. Even if they feel well, they must still test themselves at least once a day.

At the diabetes center

At the center, Sunil is weighed and measured by Rachel, a diabetes educator.

About every three months, Sunil goes to the diabetes center at the local hospital. His mom or dad goes with him. Sunil says:

"First I usually see Rachel, a diabetes educator. I like her a lot. She taught me how to use my blood glucose meter and how to fill in my record book. Rachel answers any questions me and my mom and dad have about my diabetes. She also talks to me about school and my friends. She cheers me up if I'm feeling cross about always having to remember to eat regularly.

"I also have lots of tests done at the center. First Rachel weighs and measures me. Then she looks at the places I inject myself to check the skin isn't becoming sore or lumpy. She also gives me a blood test and a urine test. On some visits she checks my blood pressure, my eyesight, and my feet. That tickles!

"Sometimes I see Joyce. She's the **dietician**. She teaches me how to eat healthily so that I keep feeling well. My mom or dad often ask her questions about what sort of foods are best for me, and how to cook meals that everyone in our family will like.

"Dr. Jacobs is an important member of my diabetes care team. He checks the results of all my tests. He also looks through my record book and tells me if I need to make any changes to my diet, or to the amount of insulin I'm taking. Usually everything is fine.

"'See you in three months!' he says."

Rachel answers any questions Sunil and his mom have about Sunil's diabetes.

Rachel and Dr. Jacobs are part of Sunil's diabetes care team.

Ups and downs

Sometimes Sunil gets fed up about his diabetes. Ahmed tries to be a good friend and cheer him up.

When Sunil first found out he had diabetes, he had to spend a few days in hospital until his blood sugar level came down. His mom stayed with him and his dad visited every day after work. The doctors and nurses explained what diabetes was, and how Sunil could learn to control it.

Since then, Sunil has hardly ever missed school. My mum says that's because Sunil eats well and gets plenty of exercise. But everyone is ill sometimes. Unlike other people, though, when Sunil is ill his glucose level

Sunil usually forgets all about his diabetes—especially when he's having fun with his friends.

often rises. It's then really important that he takes his insulin—even if he doesn't feel like eating. To stop him feeling thirsty, his mom gives him lots of sugar-free drinks. Every few hours she checks his glucose level. If his glucose level keeps rising, his mum phones his diabetes care team for advice, to see if Sunil needs to go to hospital.

Once, when Sunil had flu, he did have to go into hospital. He missed an important soccer match and was really fed up.

"Why do I have to have diabetes?" he said. "It's not fair!"

When he was back at school, I spent ages cheering him up. Most of the time though, Sunil doesn't fuss about his diabetes at all. It's just become part of his life.

Sunil tries not to eat snacks between meals, but if he's hungry he chooses something with a low sugar content.

DIABETES FACTS

A GOOD FRIEND

Everyone feels angry or disappointed about things sometimes. People with diabetes are no different. They might get fed up with injecting themselves, or having to limit how many candies or cakes they eat.

If a friend of yours has diabetes and is feeling unhappy, take time to listen. You know they'd do the same for you.

In an emergency

If a friend passes out, place them on their side, in the recovery position, and get help.

If people with diabetes don't eat enough to keep their blood glucose level above 4, they can have a serious hypoglycemia attack. If this happens they may become confused or angry, and if you try to give them something sugary to eat, they may refuse or even run away!

If a friend of yours has serious hypoglycemia, he or she may pass out.

If this happens, here is what you should do:

1. Quickly ask someone to find your friend's mom or dad and tell them what's happened. If you know your friend's parents aren't nearby, find another adult to come and help.
2. Make sure your friend is lying down, but not on their back.
3. Move any hard objects out of the way.
4. Make sure your friend is warm. Put a coat or a blanket over them if necessary.
5. Call an ambulance straight away.
6. If someone finds your friend's mom or dad, they will probably bring a tube of a glucose jelly to squirt onto your friend's gums. If your friend is still conscious and able to swallow, a couple of squirts should get enough glucose into the blood stream to make your friend come round. If your friend has passed out, they may give him or her an injection. (Injections should only be given by a parent or a paramedic.) This should have the same effect.
7. If no one can find your friend's parents, show a grown-up your friend's diabetes ID card, necklace, or bracelet, if they have one. This will tell them whom they should contact in an emergency.
8. Finally, try to keep calm and don't worry. Remember, if you follow these instructions, your friend should soon be well again.

Questions people ask

Steve Redgrave, winner of five Olympic gold medals for rowing, has diabetes.

Q. **Has anybody famous had diabetes?**
A. Yes. There's the Olympic Gold Medallist for rowing, Steve Redgrave, the actress Halle Berry, and the actor Tom Parks. Other famous people who had diabetes include the jazz trumpet player Dizzy Gillespie, the singer Ella Fitzgerald, the writer Ernest Hemingway, the Impressionist painter Cezanne, and the inventor Thomas Edison.

Q. **Do dogs and cats get diabetes?**
A. For some reason, diabetes is common among miniature poodles and cairn terriers, but not among more common breeds such as cocker spaniels, German shepherds, collies, and boxers. There's no such difference between breeds of cat.

Dogs or cats with diabetes are treated in the same way as humans—either through diet or regular doses of insulin.

Q. **Is there a cure for diabetes?**
A. No. There is no cure yet, but treatment has improved such a lot that diabetes can now be controlled so that people are less likely to develop problems with their eyes, feet, heart, and **kidneys**. Doctors are hoping to find a way to prevent Type 1 and Type 2 diabetes in the future by studying the different things that cause diabetes, and how people can **inherit** diabetes from their parents or other family members.

Children can inherit diabetes from their parents or other family members.

Q. **Can people with diabetes eat candy?**

A. Yes, in moderation—no foods are banned. Special diabetic foods are no better than ordinary foods, and eating lots of diabetic candy can cause diarrhea.

People with diabetes can eat candy and chocolate—but only in moderation.

Q. **Does eating too much sugar cause diabetes?**

A. No, although being overweight may make it more likely that someone will develop Type 2 diabetes.

Q. **Can you catch diabetes?**

A. No. Diabetes is not an infection, like a cold or the flu, so you cannot catch it.

Exercise is great fun, keeps you healthy, and stops you being overweight.

Q. **Are there any jobs you can't do if you have diabetes?**

A. Yes. At present, people with diabetes cannot usually join the armed forces or the police, fire, and ambulance services. Also, depending on their treatment, they may not be allowed to be airline pilots, train drivers, truck drivers, or taxi drivers. This is because they may cause an accident having hypoglycemia while flying a plane or driving. Diabetics may not be allowed to work offshore on oil rigs or on ocean liners.

Glossary

blood glucose meter Hand-held device to measure the amount of glucose in the blood.

carbohydrates Starchy foods (such as bread, potatoes, rice, and pasta) that release glucose slowly and steadily into the blood.

cells Tiny living parts that make up our bodies. We have millions of cells and they each do different jobs, so you have skin cells, bone cells, brain cells, and blood cells.

dietician Someone who is an expert on diet—the food we eat to stay healthy.

dose A measured amount of medicine. A doctor says how much medicine should be taken.

glucose A kind of sugar. Glucose in our bodies is needed for energy to run, walk, sleep, think, and grow.

hypoglycemia People with diabetes have hypoglycemia when sugar levels in their blood become too low. Symptoms include feeling hot or cold, sick, or tired.

inherit To be born with a physical feature, including a medical problem, that has been passed on from the parent or another family member to a child.

inject To force a liquid into the body, usually with a syringe or a similar device.

insulin A chemical made in the pancreas that controls the amount of glucose (sugar) in our blood.

kidneys Two organs in the lower part of the body which help to get rid of body waste and produce urine.

pancreas A gland near the stomach that makes a chemical called insulin.

protein Part of food that gives us energy to grow and keeps us healthy. It is found in meat, such as chicken, fish, eggs, and beans.

symptoms Something felt by a person who has an illness or disease. For example, feeling thirsty and tired are two of the symptoms of diabetes.

syringe Plastic tube with a needle at one end used to inject liquid through the skin and into the body.

Type 1 diabetes A kind of diabetes in which the pancreas does not make any insulin. Type 1 diabetes is more common in children than Type 2 diabetes. Children with Type 1 diabetes need to inject themselves with insulin for the rest of their lives.

Type 2 diabetes A kind of diabetes in which the pancreas can make some insulin but the body is not able to use the insulin properly. Type 2 is the most common kind of diabetes. It usually develops in people who are middle-aged or older. It can often be controlled by diet and by taking tablets rather than by having injections.

undiagnosed When an illness or disease has not yet been diagnosed, or identified, by recognizing the symptoms.

urine Waste fluid produced in the kidneys.

Useful organizations

HERE ARE SOME ORGANIZATIONS YOU MIGHT LIKE TO CONTACT FOR MORE INFORMATION ABOUT DIABETES

THE AMERICAN DIABETES ASSOCIATION (ADA)
1701 North Beauregard St.
Alexandria, VA 22311
www.diabetes.org
Works to improve lives of people with diabetes. Gives information, runs summer camps, publishes magazines etc.

THE JUVENILE DIABETES RESEARCH FOUNDATION
120 Wall St, New York
NY 10005-4001
www.jdrf.org
Supports research to a find a cure for juvenile diabetes. Published a "Countdown for Kids" magazine which includes finding a penpal who also has diabetes.

OTHER WEBSITES

www.diabetic.com/
Includes newsletters and recipes for people with diabetes.

www.childrenwithdiabetes.com/
Helps children with diabetes and their families learn about diabetes and meet other people with diabetes. It includes favorite recipes, tips on making blood tests and injections as easy as possible, plus help and information about diabetes at school.

www.diabetes.org/wizdom/index.shtml
Includes information, games, tips, links, and a bulletin board where children can post questions about diabetes.

www.diabetesnet.com
Has information and lets you shop online for treatments, cookbooks, etc. There are ideas for meal planning, exercise, and links to more information.

www.thehumanelement.com/courage/
Tells of the comic adventures of Courage, the superhero with diabetes, and his companion, Monitor, as they fight Courage's arch-enemy, Sugarosis.

Index